ESSENTIAL **DK** COMPUTERS

SPREADSHEETS

CREATING
WORKSHEETS

ABOUT THIS BOOK

Creating Worksheets is an easy-to-follow guide to Microsoft's spreadsheet program, Excel. This book is designed to be used by anyone who has no, or very little, experience with Excel.

XCEL'S ESSENTIAL FEATURES ARE presented in separate chapters to allow easy understanding of their functions.

The chapters and the subsections present the information using step-by-step sequences. Virtually every step is accompanied by an illustration showing how your screen should look at each stage.

Before you can do anything sophisticated with Excel, you need to know how to enter data correctly into worksheet cells. You also need to know how to change or correct this data; how to copy and move data around the worksheet; and how to insert, clear, and delete cells. The majority of this book consists of instructions for performing these essential, simple tasks. Some basic examples run through the book, and it may be difficult to keep track of these if you skip any sections. (Note: These examples are designed to illustrate various specific techniques, and do not necessarily reflect typical worksheet uses or design.)

By the end of this book, you will be able to create your own versions of Excel spreadsheets.

The book contains several features to help you understand both what is happening and what you need to do. A labeled Excel window is included to show you where to find the important elements in Excel. This is followed by an illustration of the rows of buttons, or "toolbars," at the top of the screen, to help you find your way around these invaluable, but initially perplexing, controls.

Command keys, such as ENTER and CTRL, are shown in these rectangles: [Enter ←] and [Ctrl], so that there's no confusion, for example, over whether you should press that key, or type the letters "ctrl."

Cross-references are shown in the text as left- or right-hand page icons: and . The page number and the reference are shown at the foot of the page.

As well as the step-by-step sections, there are boxes that explain a feature in detail, and tip boxes that provide alternative methods and shortcuts. Finally, at the back, you will find a glossary explaining new terms and a comprehensive index.

ESSENTIAL DK COMPUTERS

SPREADSHEETS

CREATING WORKSHEETS

ROBERT DINWIDDIE

A Dorling Kindersley Book

Dorling Kindersley
LONDON, NEW YORK, DELHI, SYDNEY

Produced for Dorling Kindersley Limited by
Design Revolution, Queens Park Villa,
30 West Drive, Brighton, East Sussex BN2 2GE

EDITORIAL DIRECTOR Ian Whitelaw
SENIOR DESIGNER Andy Ashdown
EDITOR John Watson
DESIGNER Andrew Easton

MANAGING EDITOR Sharon Lucas
SENIOR MANAGING ART EDITOR Derek Coombes
DTP DESIGNER Sonia Charbonnier
PRODUCTION CONTROLLER Wendy Penn

First American Edition, 2000

2 4 6 8 10 9 7 5 3 1

Published in the United States by Dorling Kindersley, Inc.
95 Madison Avenue, New York, New York, 10016

Published in Great Britain by Dorling Kindersley.

A catalog record is available from the Library of Congress.

ISBN 0-7894-5530-7

Color reproduced by First Impressions, London
Printed in Italy by Graphicom

For our complete
catalog visit
www.dk.com

CONTENTS

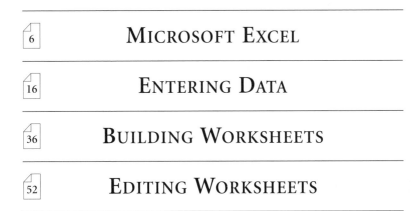

MICROSOFT EXCEL

Excel belongs to the group of computer applications known as spreadsheets, and the first spreadsheet program started the process of making computers an indispensable business tool.

WHAT CAN EXCEL DO?

Storing spreadsheet data is only the beginning as far as Excel is concerned. The wide range of features it contains let you manipulate and present your data in almost any way you choose. Excel can be an accounts program; it can be used as a sophisticated calculator capable of utilizing complex mathematical formulas; it can also be a diary, a scheduler, and more. Used in combination with Microsoft Word, Excel's database features make creating mailing lists and personalized letters very easy. Excel's presentation facilities use color, borders, and different fonts to emphasize data. A variety of charts is available, which can be selected to suit the kind of data being presented. For storing, manipulating, and presenting data, Microsoft Excel offers an unrivaled range of possibilities.

WHAT IS A WORKSHEET?

At the heart of Excel is a two-dimensional grid of data storage spaces called a worksheet (right). This is where you input the data that you want to store, manipulate, or analyze. The individual spaces are called worksheet cells. To begin with, all the cells are empty. As you put data into the cells, you build and develop the individual worksheets.

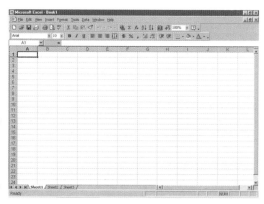

LAUNCHING EXCEL

Approaching a new program for the first time can be a daunting experience because you don't know what to expect. However, new programs are learned one step at a time and the first step is the simple one of launching Excel from your desktop.

1 LAUNCHING WITH THE START MENU

So, let's get going. First you need to launch Excel.

• If you are running Windows 95 or 98, click on the Start button at bottom left, and then choose Programs from the pop-up list. Microsoft Excel should appear in the submenu to the right (or it may be within a Microsoft Office Program group). Highlight the words Microsoft Excel and click with the mouse.

• The Excel window appears on screen .

2 LAUNCHING WITH A SHORTCUT

• If there is already a shortcut to Excel on your Desktop, just double-click on the shortcut icon.

• The Excel window appears on screen .

THE EXCEL WINDOW

Soon after you launch Microsoft Excel, a window called Microsoft Excel – Book1 appears. At the center of the window is a worksheet – a grid of blank rectangular cells. Letters and numbers label the columns and rows of the grid. Each cell has an address (such as E3), which is the column and row in which it is found.

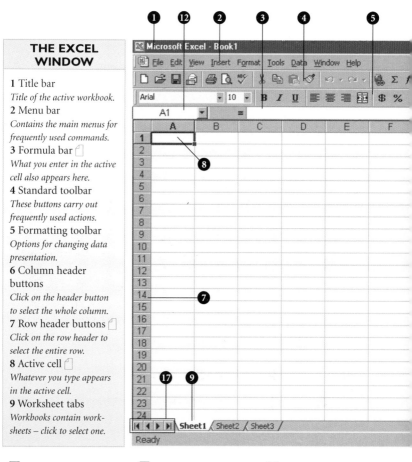

THE EXCEL WINDOW

1 Title bar
Title of the active workbook.
2 Menu bar
Contains the main menus for frequently used commands.
3 Formula bar
What you enter in the active cell also appears here.
4 Standard toolbar
These buttons carry out frequently used actions.
5 Formatting toolbar
Options for changing data presentation.
6 Column header buttons
Click on the header button to select the whole column.
7 Row header buttons
Click on the row header to select the entire row.
8 Active cell
Whatever you type appears in the active cell.
9 Worksheet tabs
Workbooks contain worksheets – click to select one.

16	Selecting Worksheet Cells	18	Selecting a single row

30	Formulas and Calculations

TOOLBAR LAYOUT

If Excel doesn't show the Formatting toolbar below the Standard toolbar, first place the cursor over the Formatting toolbar "handle." When the four-headed arrow appears, (right) hold down the mouse button and "drag" the toolbar into position.

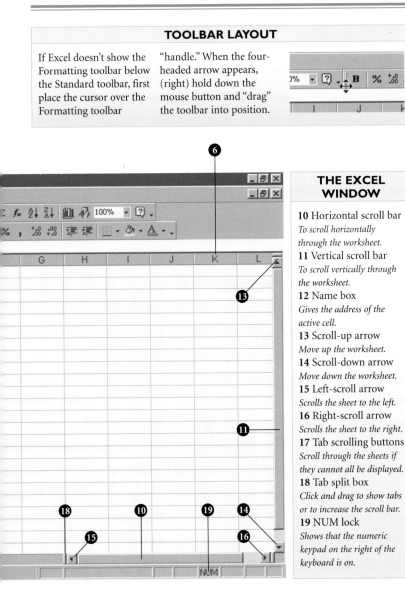

THE EXCEL WINDOW

10 Horizontal scroll bar
To scroll horizontally through the worksheet.

11 Vertical scroll bar
To scroll vertically through the worksheet.

12 Name box
Gives the address of the active cell.

13 Scroll-up arrow
Move up the worksheet.

14 Scroll-down arrow
Move down the worksheet.

15 Left-scroll arrow
Scrolls the sheet to the left.

16 Right-scroll arrow
Scrolls the sheet to the right.

17 Tab scrolling buttons
Scroll through the sheets if they cannot all be displayed.

18 Tab split box
Click and drag to show tabs or to increase the scroll bar.

19 NUM lock
Shows that the numeric keypad on the right of the keyboard is on.

THE TWO MAIN EXCEL TOOLBARS

Many of the actions, or commands, that you want to perform on data can be carried out by clicking on toolbar buttons. When you launch Excel, the Standard toolbar and the Formatting toolbar are the usual toolbars displayed. They contain

buttons whose actions are described below. The Standard toolbar contains buttons for actions as diverse as opening a new workbook or undoing an action. The Formatting toolbar contains buttons for changing the worksheet's appearance.

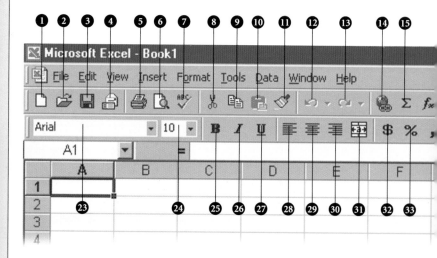

BUTTON FUNCTIONS

1 New workbook	9 Copy	17 Sort ascending
2 Open file	10 Paste	18 Sort descending
3 Save workbook	11 Format painter	19 Chart wizard
4 E-mail workbook/sheet	12 Undo action(s)	20 Drawing toolbar
5 Print	13 Redo action(s)	21 Zoom view
6 Print preview	14 Insert hyperlink	22 Help
7 Spelling checker	15 AutoSum	23 Font selector
8 Cut	16 Paste function	24 Font size selector

 14 Opening a new workbook

41 Copying and Pasting

 56 Checking Spelling

CUSTOMIZING A TOOLBAR

Click the arrow at far right of the Formatting toolbar then on the arrow on the Add or Remove Buttons box that appears. A drop-down menu opens from which you can add or remove toolbar buttons.

ScreenTips
It isn't necessary to memorize all these buttons. Roll the cursor over a button, wait for a second, and a ScreenTip appears telling you the function of the button.

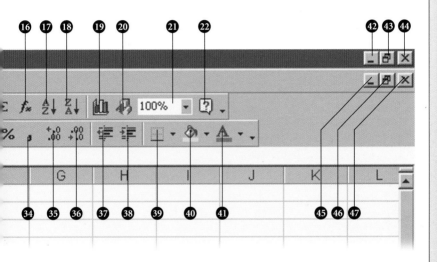

BUTTON FUNCTIONS

25 Bold	**33** Percent style	**41** Font color
26 Italic	**34** Comma style	**42** Minimize Excel
27 Underline	**35** Increase decimals	**43** Restore Excel
28 Aligned left	**36** Decrease decimals	**44** Close Excel
29 Center	**37** Decrease indent	**45** Minimize worksheet
30 Align right	**38** Increase indent	**46** Restore worksheet
31 Merge and center	**39** Add/remove borders	**47** Close worksheet
32 Currency style	**40** Fill color	

 25 Entering decimal numbers

 34 Adding a border

 35 Highlighting information

NAMING, SAVING, AND FINDING WORKBOOKS

Anything you create using Microsoft Excel is stored on your computer as a file called a workbook. A workbook contains one or more separate worksheets. When you first start up Excel, you are presented with an unused workbook called Book1. This contains from 3 to 10 blank worksheets, depending on the version of Excel. The blank worksheets are initially called Sheet1, Sheet2, and so on.

1 RENAMING A WORKSHEET

• You can switch between worksheets by clicking on the tabs at the bottom of the workbook window. To begin with, the worksheets are all blank.

Once you put data into a worksheet, you should give the worksheet a short name to indicate what it contains. Because all worksheets start with a default name (like Sheet1), you are actually renaming the worksheet. Here's how to do it.

• Double-click on the existing name, so that it becomes highlighted.

• Type the new name and press [Enter ←].

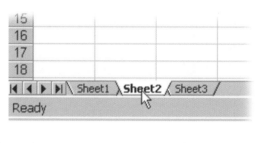

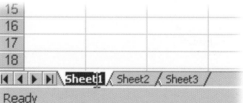

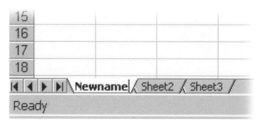

2 SAVING AND NAMING

You should save your work frequently. Saving means copying to your computer's hard disk. When you save in Excel, you save the whole workbook containing the worksheet(s) that you have been developing.

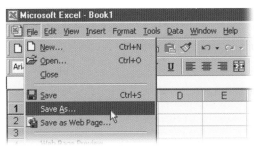

The first time you save a workbook, you should name it (actually rename it) at the same time.

● Choose Save As from the File menu.

● The Save As dialog box appears. Your workbook will be saved in the folder displayed in the Save in box. In this instance, just accept the displayed folder. Remember the name of the folder in which you've saved the workbook.

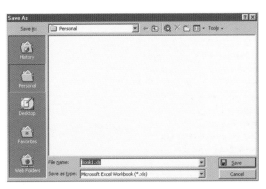

● In the File name box, type the name you would like to give your workbook (Excel will automatically add the extension .xls). Then click on the Save button.

● On subsequent occasions when you want to save the workbook, just click the Save button on the Standard toolbar.

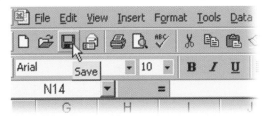

3 CLOSING A WORKBOOK

• Click the close button at top right.

• If you have made any changes since your last save, a box appears asking whether you want to save changes. Click Yes (or No if you do not wish to save any changes you've made).

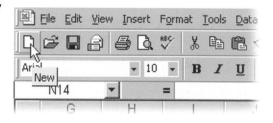

4 OPENING A NEW WORKBOOK

Just click the new workbook button on the Standard toolbar.

5 OPEN A SAVED WORKBOOK

• Click the Open button on the Standard toolbar

• In the Open dialog box, click on the workbook you want to open.

• Click on the Open button at bottom right of the box.

6 FIND A SAVED WORKBOOK

After you have been using Excel for some time, there will be occasions when you cannot find the workbook you want. Excel contains its own find file facility to help you when this happens.

• To find a workbook, begin by clicking on Open in the File menu, click on Tools at top right in the Open dialog box and choose Find.

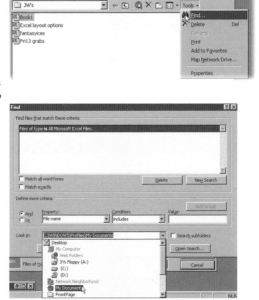

• The Find dialog box opens. Drop down the Look in: menu and select the area to search – in this case, the folder called My documents. Click in the Search subfolders check box if necessary, and click on Find now.

• The Open window reappears with the list of Excel workbooks that have been found.

ENTERING DATA

The Excel program is based on the worksheet – a grid of individual boxes, or "cells," into which you enter data. You can then manipulate that data in various ways.

SELECTING WORKSHEET CELLS

Before performing any operation in Excel – for example, typing data into cells, coloring cells, or deleting them – you need to choose which cells you are going to perform the action on. This process is called cell selection and is a fundamental Excel skill. You can select a single cell, a block of cells, a horizontal row or vertical column, or several rows or columns at the same time. You can also select several groups of cells. When a group of cells is selected, they will appear in black, except for one cell, the "active cell" (see box below), which remains white. Try practicing these techniques following the instructions below.

1 SELECTING A SINGLE CELL

• Move the mouse pointer over your chosen cell and click the left mouse button.
• The thick black border that now appears around the cell indicates that it is selected, and this is now the active cell.

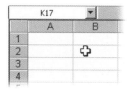

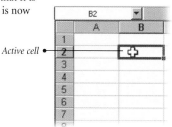

Active cell •

ACTIVE CELLS

The significance of the active cell is that once you have made a selection, anything you type will appear only in the active cell. Other actions that you perform after selection (such as coloring cells or deleting them) will apply to all the cells in the selected area.

WHY SELECT MULTIPLE CELLS?

You select multiple cells most often to perform "block" activities such as formatting, inserting new columns, rows, and cells, clearing cells, or duplicating existing data from a single cell to several cells. New data can be typed into cells only one cell at a time (in the outlined or "active" cell), but it sometimes saves time to select all the cells into which you are going to enter data before you start typing. You can easily move the active cell around in the selected area one cell at a time using the [Tab⇆] key.

2 SELECTING A BLOCK OF CELLS

A block can range from a few adjacent cells in a single row or column to a large rectangular area.
• Click on a cell at one end (or at one corner) of the block you wish to select.
• Hold down the [⇧ Shift] key, and then click on the cell at the opposite end (or corner) of the block.

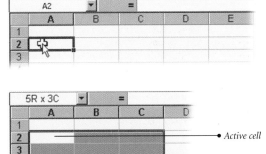

● *Active cell*

3 SELECTING A SINGLE COLUMN

• Click on the column header button at the top of your chosen column.

Column header button ●

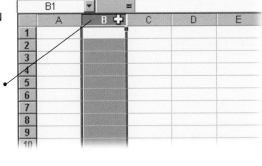

4 SELECTING A SINGLE ROW

• Click on the row header button to the left of your chosen row. This row will then be highlighted.

Row header button •

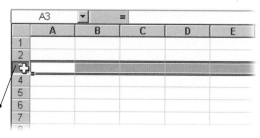

5 SELECTING ROWS OR COLUMNS

• While holding down the left-hand mouse button, drag the mouse pointer across the header buttons for the columns or rows you wish to include, and then release the button.

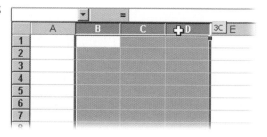

6 SELECTING SEVERAL BLOCKS

• Select the first cell or block, hold down the [Ctrl] key, select the next cell or block, then select a third cell or block, and so on. Release the [Ctrl] key only when you have completed your selections.

Active cell •

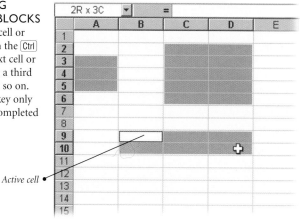

7 SELECTING ALL THE WORKSHEET

• Click on the top left corner of the border of the worksheet. This is called the Select All button. The whole of the worksheet will now be highlighted, and the top left cell is the active cell.

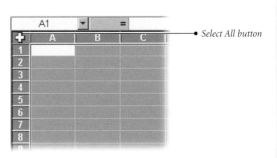

• *Select All button*

ENTERING TEXT

There are three categories of data that you can put into a worksheet – text, numbers, and formulas. Worksheets usually take a tabular form, and text is used most often as labels for the table's rows and columns. It makes sense to enter these text labels first, in order to provide a structure for the numerical data and formulas. To learn the techniques for entering data, you may find

it helpful to follow a worked example. The example given here involves creating a sales worksheet for a small business, Fantasy Ices, that makes ice cream products. Alternatively, you can use the same methods for any worksheet you choose. To follow the example, open a new workbook and save it as **fantasyices.xls**. Rename Sheet1 in the workbook **Sales**.

1 SELECT THE FIRST CELL FOR TEXT

Click on cell A2 to select this cell. Cell A2 is now the active cell and anything you type on the keyboard will appear in this cell. Note that A2 appears in the name box to the top left of the worksheet.

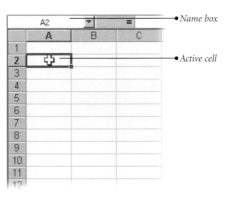

• *Name box*

• *Active cell*

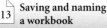

| 13 | **Saving and naming a workbook** | 12 | **Renaming a worksheet** |

2 TYPING IN THE TEXT

For the worked example, type the word **Product**. Note that a flashing bar, called the insertion point, stays just to the right of the last letter you typed, marking where the next letter you type will appear. Don't worry for now if you make typing mistakes.

• Insertion point

Oops... typing error

If you mistype a letter, press the ← Bksp key on your keyboard to delete the last letter you typed. If you want to start data entry into a cell from scratch, press the Esc key. Even if you have completed entering data, it's easy to change data later ⌐.

3 COMPLETE THE ENTRY

• Once you have typed your text, press Enter ↵. This completes the data entry into the cell, and the active cell now moves down a single cell to A3.

4 LABELS FOR ROW HEADINGS

• Into cell A3, type **Twizzlesticks** – this is the company's biggest product. Press Enter ↵.
• Repeat the process by typing **Chokky bars**, **Orange sorbet**, and **Raspberry surprise** into cells A4, A5, and A6. These are the company's other three products. Press Enter ↵ after typing each of these text labels.

52 Changing Cell Contents

5 COLUMN HEADING TEXT

Now add some further text labels as column headers for the numerical data you are going to enter into the worksheet.

● Select cells B2 to D2 (see page 17 to remind yourself how to select). Type **Sales (boxes)**, which appears in the active cell, B2.

● Complete the entry by pressing the Tab⇆ key. This time, the active cell moves one cell to the right.

● Type **Price ($)** into C2, press the Tab⇆ key, and type **Sales Revenue** into D2.

B2	▼ ✕ ✓ =	Sales (boxes		
	A	B	C	D	E
1					
2	Product	Sales (boxes			
3	Twizzlesticks				
4	Chokky bars				
5	Orange sorbet				⇩
6	Raspberry surprise				
7					

	▼ ✕ ✓ =	Price ($)		
	A	B	C	D	E
1					
2	Product	Sales (box	Price ($)		
3	Twizzlesticks				
4	Chokky bars				
5	Orange sorbet				
6	Raspberry surprise				
7					

Overflowing text

When you type a long text label into a cell, it may appear to overflow into the next cell on the right – and when you type into that next cell, your long text label appears to have been cut off. Don't worry – it's easy to fix. There are several ways of adjusting the width of columns so that all the text fits 🗋.

TEXT ALIGNMENT

Note that Excel will automatically start any text label at the left-hand end of the cell (the text is said to be ranged left) whereas numerical values are ranged right. Excel classifies anything typed into a cell as text unless it specifically recognizes it as a numerical value. You can change the alignment of data in a cell using toolbar buttons 🗋.

| 23 | **Adjusting the column width** |
| 10 | **The Two Main Excel Toolbars** |

6 ADD FURTHER TEXT LABELS

• Select cell C7 and type **Total Revenue**. Press Enter↵ when finished.
• Select cell B10 and type **Last Updated**. Press Enter↵, type **Date** into cell B11, press Enter↵, and type **Time** into the B12 cell.
• Select cell A14 and type **Proportion of our products that are**. Press Enter↵ and type the text labels shown at bottom right into cells A15 to A17. When you type **Ice milk** in cell A17, Excel may suggest that you want to enter the label **Ice cream** in this cell. Ignore this and just keep typing.

	A	B	C	D	E
			C7	▼ X ✓ = Total Revenue	
1					
2	Product	Sales (box	Price ($)	Sales Revenue	
3	Twizzlesticks				
4	Chokky bars				
5	Orange sorbet				
6	Raspberry surprise				
7			Total Revenue		
8					
9					
10					

A17 ▼ X ✓ = Ice milk

	A	B	C	D	E
1					
2	Product	Sales (box	Price ($)	Sales Revenue	
3	Twizzlesticks				
4	Chokky bars				
5	Orange sorbet				
6	Raspberry surprise				
7			Total Revenue		
8					
9					
10		Last Updated			
11		Date			

9			
10		Last Updated	
11		Date	
12		Time	
13			
14	Proportion of our products that are		
15	Ice cream		
16	Sorbets		
17	Ice milk		
18			
19			
20			
21			

COMPLETION KEYS

There are various keyboard methods for completing the entry of data into a cell. In addition to the Enter↵ and Tab⇥ keys (which move the active cell down or to the right, respectively, on completing the entry), you can use the cursor arrow keys for moving the active cell in various directions as you complete an entry.

7 ADJUST THE COLUMN WIDTHS

There are some quick methods for adjusting the widths of columns to fit cell data. For this example:

• Move the mouse pointer over the line that divides column headers A and B. The pointer should form a bar with arrows pointing to either side.

• Press down on the left mouse button, and drag the mouse pointer to the right. A dotted vertical line shows the position of the new column divider. Release the mouse button when it is to the right of the words **Raspberry surprise** in cell A6, and the column widens to that extent.

• With the mouse pointer on the line that divides column headers B and C, double-click the mouse. This method automatically widens column B to display the longest line of text in that column. Now widen columns C and D.

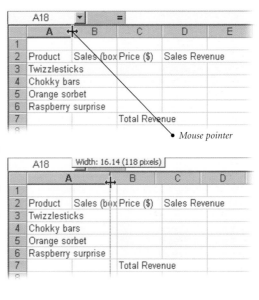

Mouse pointer

AUTOCOMPLETE

You will often need to enter the same text label more than once into a worksheet. If Excel detects that you have started typing a text label for the second time into the same column, the handy Autocomplete feature supplies the text for you, highlighted in black. To accept the autocompleted text, press [Enter ←] (or [Tab ⇆]). To ignore it, just carry on typing.

ENTERING NUMBERS

Numerical values include integers (whole numbers), decimal numbers (such as 3.25), fractions, monetary amounts, percentages, dates, and times. Excel applies various rules to detect whether a string of characters typed into a cell constitute a numerical value and, if so, what types

(integer, date, time etc). If Excel recognizes the typed-in expression as a numerical value, it will align it ranged right in the cell. Excel can perform a calculation on the contents of a cell only if it has been entered and recognized as a numerical value.

1 ENTERING WHOLE NUMBERS

Just click on the cell that you wish to hold the number and then type.

• In the case of our worked example, click on cell B3 and type in any whole number between 1,000 and 10,000. These are the sales of boxes of Twizzlesticks. You can choose whether or not to type commas in numbers above 1,000. Press Enter↵ to complete the entry once you have typed your number.

• Now enter further whole numbers (less than 1,000) into cells B4 to B6, pressing Enter↵ after each entry. These numbers represent the sales of boxes of the company's other products.

	B3	▼	X ✓ =	3467
	A	B	C
1			
2	Product	Sales (boxes)	Price ($)	Sale
3	Twizzlesticks	3467	
4	Chokky bars		
5	Orange sorbet		
6	Raspberry surprise		

	B6	▼	=	345
	A	B	C
1			
2	Product	Sales (boxes)	Price ($)	Sale
3	Twizzlesticks	3467	
4	Chokky bars	893	
5	Orange sorbet	98	
6	Raspberry surprise	345	

IS IT A NUMBER?

Excel interprets various sorts of expression (not just strings of digits) as numerical values. For example $43, or 43%, or 4.3, or 4,300, or 4.3E+7

(standing for 43,000,000) are all recognized as numerical values. Both −43 and (43) would be recognized as negative or debit numbers.

NUMBER FORMATS

The way in which a number or numerical expression is displayed in a cell is affected by what format that cell has. By default, cells have a "general" number format. When you type any numerical expression into a cell that has this "general" number format,
Excel analyzes what type of expression it is and then displays it in an appropriate standard way, usually (though not always exactly) as it is typed. For example, an integer will be displayed as an integer, a date will be given a date format, and so on.

2 ENTERING DECIMALS

You enter decimal numbers into cells just as you would write them. Simply type a period to represent the decimal point.

• For the worked example, select cell C3 in the Price column, and type a decimal number, such as **6.25**. This is the price of a box of Twizzlesticks, with cents after the decimal point (you'll apply a $ sign later). Press Enter ←.

• A box of Chokky bars is priced at only 74 cents, so enter **0.74** in cell C4 and press Enter ←. Orange sorbet is a big ticket item at $21.33 a box, so type **21.33** in cell C5.

C3	▼ X ✓ =	6.25	
	A	B	C	Sale
1				
2	Product	Sales (boxes)	Price ($)	Sale
3	Twizzlesticks	3467	6.25	
4	Chokky bars	893		
5	Orange sorbet	98		
6	Raspberry surprise	345		
7			Total Revenue	
8				
9				

C4	▼ X ✓ =	0.74	
	A	B	C	Sale
1				
2	Product	Sales (boxes)	Price ($)	Sale
3	Twizzlesticks	3467	6.25	
4	Chokky bars	893	0.74	
5	Orange sorbet	98		
6	Raspberry surprise	345		
7			Total Revenue	
8				
9				
10		Last Updated		
11		Date		
12		Time		

3 ENTERING FRACTIONS

For fractions, you type the two parts of the fraction divided by a / (forward slash).

• A box of Raspberry surprise ices has the rather curious price tag of $12¾. In cell C6, type the fraction **12 3/4**, i.e., type a 1, a 2, a space, a 3, then a forward slash, and finally a 4. Then press Enter⏎ .

	A	B	C	
			C6 ▾ ✕ ✓ = 12 3/4	
1				
2	Product	Sales (boxes)	Price ($)	Sale
3	Twizzlesticks	3467	6.25	
4	Chokky bars	893	0.74	
5	Orange sorbet	98	21.33	
6	Raspberry surprise	345	12 3/4	
7			Total Revenue	
8				
9				
10		Last Updated		
11		Date		
12		Time		

LONG NUMBERS

If you enter a number that is more than 11 digits long into a cell, it is displayed in abbreviated scientific notation. For example, if you type 3,287,600,000,000, on completing the entry it will be displayed as 3.2876E+12. This means 3.2876×10^{12}. If you want the number to be displayed in full, you must change the format of the cell from the general to the number format. To do this, select the cell, choose Cells from the Format menu, click on Number under Category in the Format Cells dialog box, and then click on OK. You may then see a series of ###s in the cell, indicating that your number does not fit in the cell. To fix this, you must widen ⃞ the cell.

ENTERING CURRENCY AND DATES

You can enter monetary amounts into cells by typing the appropriate currency symbol ($ or £) before the number representing the amount. Alternatively it can save time to enter all the amounts without symbols, and then apply the Currency Style to all the appropriate cells. A Style is a set of formats (attributes that define how the contents of a cell look or behave). In the case of the Currency Style, this is a very simple set of formats that can be applied with one click of a toolbar button, as you will see. To enter dates and times, you should follow certain conventions to make sure what you type is recorded correctly as a date or time.

23 **Adjusting the column width**

1 ENTERING CURRENCY

In the worked example, you have already entered the product prices in column C. Here's how to apply the Currency Style.
• Select cells C3 to C6.
• Click on the Currency Style button on the Formatting toolbar.
• A $ sign is added before each product price.

SINGLE CURRENCY

For Excel to recognize a monetary amount as a number, you are limited to using the currency defined under Regional Settings in your system's Control Panel (normally $ in the US and £ in the UK). If the default symbol is $, typing £35, for example, will not be recognized as a numerical value (but you can change the default if you wish). Cell entries that are not recognized as numerical values cannot be used in Excel calculations.

16 **Selecting Worksheet Cells**

2 ENTERING DATES

A standard way for entering a date into a cell so that it will be recognized as a date is to type the day, a space, the first three letters of the month, a space, then the year in full.

• Select cell C11, type **7 Jun 2000** and press Enter ←.

• The entry is displayed in the cell as 7-Jun-00, ranged right indicating that it has been recognized as a date.

C11	▼	X ✓ =	7 Jun 2000	
	A	B	C	
1				
2	Product	Sales (boxes)	Price ($)	Sale
3	Twizzlesticks	3467	$ 6.25	
4	Chokky bars	893	$ 0.74	
5	Orange sorbet	98	$ 21.33	
6	Raspberry surprise	345	$ 12.75	
7			Total Revenue	
8				
9				
10		Last Updated		
11		Date	7 Jun 2000	
12		Time		

Today's the Day

There is a quick way of entering today's date (as held by your PC's internal clock) into a cell. Select the cell and then press the Ctrl key and ; (semicolon) keys together.

C12	▼	=		
	A	B	C	
1				
2	Product	Sales (boxes)	Price ($)	Sale
3	Twizzlesticks	3467	$ 6.25	
4	Chokky bars	893	$ 0.74	
5	Orange sorbet	98	$ 21.33	
6	Raspberry surprise	345	$ 12.75	
7			Total Revenue	
8				
9				
10		Last Updated		
11		Date	7-Jun-00	
12		Time		
13				

MAKE A DATE!

An alternative way of entering a date is to type the month as a number, the day, then the year, separated by forward slashes, i.e. 6/7/2000 to indicate 7 June 2000. If you were to type June 7 2000, on the other hand, it would not be recognized as a date or, in fact, as any type of numerical expression. Note also that what is displayed in the cells is not always exactly what you typed. Once Excel has recognized what category a numerical value falls into, it sometimes displays it in a standard format for that category rather than showing the figures exactly as typed.

3 ENTERING TIMES

To enter a time in Excel, type the hour (using the 24-hour clock), a colon, then the minutes past the hour. Alternatively type the hour (using the 12-hour clock), a colon, the minutes past the hour, a space, and then either AM or PM.

9			
10		Last Updated	
11		Date	7-Jun-00
12		Time	15:45
13			
14	Proportion of our products that are		
15	Ice cream		
16	Sorbets		

• Into cell E12, type **15:45** and then press [Enter↵].

• Excel displays the time in the cell exactly as you have typed it in.

9			
10		Last Updated	
11		Date	7-Jun-00
12		Time	15:45
13			
14	Proportion of our products that are		
15	Ice cream		
16	Sorbets		

4 ENTERING PERCENTAGES

To enter a percentage, just type a number followed by the percentage sign. You can also convert a decimal number in a cell to a percentage by applying the Percent Style to a cell.

9			
10		Last Updated	
11		Date	7-Jun-00
12		Time	15:45
13			
14	Proportion of our products that are		
15	Ice cream	50%	
16	Sorbets		
17	Ice milk		

• Type **50%** into cell B15 and press [Enter↵].

• Type **0.25** into cell B16 and press [Enter↵].

• Click on B16 again, then click on the Percent Style button on the Formatting toolbar to convert the decimal to a percentage. Press [Enter↵]. Type **25%** into cell B17, and then save the workbook 🗋.

	%	,	+.0 .00	.00 →.0

Percent Style

9			
10		Last Updat⸱	
11		Date	
12		Time	
13			
14	Proportion of our products that are		
15	Ice cream	50%	
16	Sorbets	0.25	
17	Ice milk		
18			
19			
20			

13	**Saving and naming a workbook**

FORMULAS AND CALCULATIONS

For even the simplest Excel worksheets, you will soon want to use formulas. A formula returns (calculates and displays) a value in a cell based on numbers you supply it with, arithmetic operators (such as plus or multiply), and cell references (the numerical values held in other worksheet cells). Much of the power of Excel derives from the use of cell references in formulas, because if you decide later on to change a value in a referenced cell, all formulas in the worksheet that depend on that reference are automatically recalculated.

1 MULTIPLYING TWO CELL VALUES

• If you want a cell to contain the result of multiplying the values of two other cells, you can type an = sign into the cell followed by the addresses of the two referenced cells, separated by the multiplication operator: *.

• In the ice cream sales worksheet, you want cell D3 to contain the revenue from Twizzlestick sales. This is the sales figure (cell B3) multiplied by the price per box (cell C3). So, select cell D3 and type: = **B3*C3**. Press Enter ↵ .

• Select cell D3 again and look at the Formula bar. Note that there is a distinction between what D3 actually contains (a formula, as shown in the Formula bar) and what it displays (the value that is calculated by that formula).

SUM	▼	X ✓ =	=B3*C3	
	A	B	C	D
1				
2	Product	Sales (boxes)	Price ($)	Sales Revenue
3	Twizzlesticks	3467	$ 6.25	=B3*C3
4	Chokky bars	893	$ 0.74	
5	Orange sorbet	98	$ 21.33	
6	Raspberry surprise	345	$ 12.75	
7			Total Revenue	
8				
9				
10		Last Updated		
11		Date	7-Jun-00	
12		Time	15:45	
13				
14	Proportion of our products that are			
15	Ice cream	50%		
16	Sorbets	25%		

D3	▼	=	=B3*C3	
	A	B	C	D
1				
2	Product	Sales (boxes)	Price ($)	Sales Revenue
3	Twizzlesticks	3467	$ 6.25	$ 21,668.75
4	Chokky bars	893	$ 0.74	
5	Orange sorbet	98	$ 21.33	
6	Raspberry surprise	345	$ 12.75	
7			Total Revenue	
8				
9				
10		Last Updated		
11		Date	7-Jun-00	
12		Time	15:45	
13				
14	Proportion of our products that are			
15	Ice cream	50%		
16	Sorbets	25%		

2 FORMULAS USING THE MOUSE

• Instead of typing, you can use the mouse to help you construct formulas. Try this method for entering the formula: =B4*C4 into cell D4.

• Select cell D4 and type the = sign.

• Now click on cell B4. D4 now contains the expression: =**B4**.

• Type an asterisk (*) and then click on cell C4. Finally, press Enter↵.

	A	B	C	D
1				
2	Product	Sales (boxes)	Price ($)	Sales Revenue
3	Twizzlesticks	3467	$ 6.25	$ 21,668.75
4	Chokky bars	893	$ 0.74	=
5	Orange sorbet	98	$ 21.33	
6	Raspberry surprise	345	$ 12.75	
7			Total Revenue	
8				

	A	B	C	D
1				
2	Product	Sales (boxes)	Price ($)	Sales Revenue
3	Twizzlesticks	3467	$ 6.25	$ 21,668.75
4	Chokky bars	893	$ 0.74	=B4
5	Orange sorbet	98	$ 21.33	
6	Raspberry surprise	345	$ 12.75	
7			Total Revenue	
8				

Tip of the iceberg

Excel formulas and functions are so useful and important that a separate *Essential DK Computers* guide will shortly be available on this subject.

	A	B	C	D
1				
2	Product	Sales (boxes)	Price ($)	Sales Revenue
3	Twizzlesticks	3467	$ 6.25	$ 21,668.75
4	Chokky bars	893	$ 0.74	=B4*C4
5	Orange sorbet	98	$ 21.33	
6	Raspberry surprise	345	$ 12.75	
7			Total Revenue	
8				

3 COMPLETING THE FORMULAS

• Now use either entry method to enter the formulas: =**B5*C5** into cell D5 and: =**B6*C6** into cell D6.

	A	B	C	D
1				
2	Product	Sales (boxes)	Price ($)	Sales Revenue
3	Twizzlesticks	3467	$ 6.25	$ 21,668.75
4	Chokky bars	893	$ 0.74	$ 660.82
5	Orange sorbet	98	$ 21.33	=B5*C5
6	Raspberry surprise	345	$ 12.75	
7			Total Revenue	
8				

4 ADDING VALUES IN SEVERAL CELLS

• To add the values in several cells, you can type an addition formula. For example, to add together the sums in cells D3 to D6, you could use the formula: =D3+D4+D5+D6. However, when (as here) all the cells you want to add are adjacent in the same row or column, there is a quicker method – called AutoSum.

• In cell D7, you want to put the sum of the revenues generated by the individual products, held in cells D3 to D6. To do so, select cell D7, and then click the AutoSum button on the Standard toolbar.

• A flashing border appears around cells D3 to D6, and the term: =SUM(D3:D6) appears in cell D7 and in the formula bar. This indicates that a function (a special type of formula) called SUM, which adds the values in cells D3 to D6, is ready to be used in cell D7.

THE EXPONENTIAL OPERATOR

The exponential operator, ^, raises a value to a given power. For example, if you type: =A3^2 into a cell, Excel will take the value in cell A3 and square it. If you type: =A3^3, Excel will cube the value in cell A3. The exponential operator takes precedence over all other operators in Excel.

ARITHMETIC OPERATORS

The five arithmetic operators available are: + (addition), - (subtraction), * (multiplication), / (division), and ^ (raising to the power). These follow the standard order of operations, which can be overruled only by using brackets. For example, if you want to subtract A2 from 5, and then multiply the result by B2, you should type: =(5-A2)*B2.

• Press Enter ↵ , and the figure for total revenue appears in cell D7.

D8		=		
	A	B	C	D
1				
2	Product	Sales (boxes)	Price ($)	Sales Revenue
3	Twizzlesticks	3467	$ 6.25	$ 21,668.75
4	Chokky bars	893	$ 0.74	$ 660.82
5	Orange sorbet	98	$ 21.33	$ 2,090.34
6	Raspberry surprise	345	$ 12.75	$ 4,398.75
7			Total Revenue	$ 28,818.66
8				

QUICK CALCULATIONS

Excel can be used for one-off calculations. If you want to perform a quick calculation and you don't have a calculator, you can use any cell in Excel instead. Suppose you want to add 23 to 31 and multiply the result by 27. Select a blank cell and type: =(23+31)*27, then press Enter ↵ . If you don't want to leave your calculation on display, you should then clear the cell ▯.

SIMPLE FORMATTING

Even the most elementary worksheets may benefit from some basic formatting to help clarify which parts are headings and which are data, and to improve the visual attractiveness of the worksheet. The full range of Excel's formatting features could be the subject of a book in itself. The examples given below are some simple formatting ideas that can be applied with buttons on the Formatting toolbar.

1 EMPHASIZING HEADINGS

It is common to distinguish column and row labels. One way of doing this is to emphasize them by using a bold, colored typeface.

• Select cells A2 to D2. Hold down the Ctrl key, and then click on cell B10.

B10		= Last Updated		
	A	B	C	D
1				
2	Product	Sales (boxes)	Price ($)	Sales Revenue
3	Twizzlesticks	3467	$ 6.25	$ 21,668.75
4	Chokky bars	893	$ 0.74	$ 660.82
5	Orange sorbet	98	$ 21.33	$ 2,090.34
6	Raspberry surprise	345	$ 12.75	$ 4,398.75
7			Total Revenue	$ 28,818.66
8				
9				
10		Last Updated		
11		Date	7-Jun-00	

65 Clearing Cells

- Click the Bold button on the Formatting toolbar.
- Now click the arrow next to the Font Color button.
- Choose a shade of blue from the palette.
- Now select cells A3 to A6 and A15 to A17, and also make them bold, but using a different color.

Font Color button •

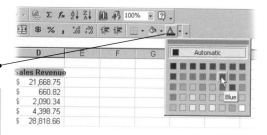

	A	B	C	D	E
		B10	=	Last Updated	
1			Bold		
2	Product	Sales (boxes)	Price ($)	Sales Revenue	
3	Twizzlesticks	3467	$ 6.25	$ 21,668.75	

	D
	Sales Revenue
	$ 21,668.75
	$ 660.82
	$ 2,090.34
	$ 4,398.75
	$ 28,818.66

READY-MADE FORMATS

For some formatting ideas, select the whole table and choose the AutoFormat command from the Format menu. In the AutoFormat dialog box, browse through the options. If you like one, choose it and then click on OK.

	A15	=	Ice cream	
	A	B	C	D
1				
2	Product	Sales (boxes)	Price ($)	Sales Revenue
3	Twizzlesticks	3467	$ 6.25	$ 21,668.75
4	Chokky bars	893	$ 0.74	$ 660.82
5	Orange sorbet	98	$ 21.33	$ 2,090.34
6	Raspberry surprise	345	$ 12.75	$ 4,398.75
7			Total Revenue	$ 28,818.66
8				
9				
10		Last Updated		

2 ADDING A BORDER

You can separate off distinct parts of a worksheet with a border. Here it would make sense to put a line under the main product sales data.

- Select cells B6 to D6.
- Click the small arrow next to the Borders button.
- Choose a thick bottom border from the palette.

	B6	=	345	
	A	B	C	D
1				
2	Product	Sales (boxes)	Price ($)	Sales Revenue
3	Twizzlesticks	3467	$ 6.25	$ 21,668.75
4	Chokky bars	893	$ 0.74	$ 660.82
5	Orange sorbet	98	$ 21.33	$ 2,090.34
6	Raspberry surprise	345	$ 12.75	$ 4,398.75
7			Total Revenue	$ 28,818.66
8				
9				
10		Last Updated		
11		Date	7-Jun-00	
12		Time	15:45	
13				
14	Proportion of our products that are			

TRANSFERRING FORMATS

You can copy a format from one cell to another without affecting the cell's contents. Select the cell whose format you want to copy, click the Format Painter button (a paintbrush) on the Standard toolbar, then click in the cell to which you want the copied format transferred.

Fill Color button

3 HIGHLIGHTING INFORMATION

It is often worth highlighting important information with a background color.

• Select cell D7, which represents Fantasy Ices' revenue to date.

• Click the small down arrow to the right of the Fill Color button.

• Choose a light shade from the palette.

BUILDING WORKSHEETS

To build Excel worksheets fast and easily, you need to know about methods for copying data, creating simple data series, and adding new rows, columns, and cells to your worksheet.

COPYING DATA BY FILLING

Putting the same data into adjacent cells is a common Excel task. Instead of typing the data into every cell, you can type it once, and then copy it by using methods called Fill and AutoFill. To practice these techniques, here's an example, which consists of setting up an appointment diary for the directors of Fantasy Ices. Open the "fantasyices.xls" workbook, click on Sheet2 and rename this sheet **Diary**.

1 ENTER SOME TEXT LABELS

Into cell A1, type **Morning Appointments July 31-August 4**. Type **Director** into cell A2, **Mr. Twizz** into cell A4, and **Mrs. Stick** into cell A11.

2 SELECT A RANGE OF CELLS TO FILL

To perform a fill, select the cell(s) you want to copy, then extend the selection into the cells where you want the copied data to appear. In this case, you want to copy Mr. Twizz into cells A5 to A8, so select the whole range A4 to A8.

NO MULTIPLE SELECTIONS

You cannot use Fill or AutoFill to copy data from a single cell (or range of cells) to multiple nonadjacent cells or ranges of cells. You can only fill data into groups of adjacent cells.

3 USE THE FILL COMMAND

● Choose Fill from the Edit menu. A submenu appears to the right of the Fill command. Choose Down from the Fill submenu.
● The range of cells from A4 to A8 now fills with the name of Mr. Twizz.

4 SELECT A CELL FOR AUTOFILL

An alternative to Fill is AutoFill, which involves dragging the mouse rather than choosing a menu command.
● Select the cell or cells that you want to copy, in this example, cell A11 (Mrs. Stick).
● At the bottom right-hand corner of the selected cell is a square called the fill handle. Move the mouse pointer over the fill handle until it becomes a cross. Now hold down the mouse button.

● *Fill handle*

FILLING A BLOCK OF CELLS

You cannot fill from a single cell into a block of cells (2 cells wide x 2 cells deep or bigger) in a single operation. Two operations are required to do this. First select the range into which data is to be copied, making sure that the cell containing the data to be copied is at one corner. Then choose a sequence of commands, such as Fill Down followed by Fill Right.

5 DEFINE THE FILL RANGE

Move the mouse pointer around the worksheet. You will see that different ranges of adjacent cells are surrounded by a border. This is the range into which your cell selection will be copied. Drag the mouse until the border surrounds the range A11 to A15.

6 COMPLETE THE AUTOFILL

Now release the mouse button. The label Mrs. Stick is copied from cell A11 into cells A12 to A15.

FILLING IN ALL DIRECTIONS

The Fill command allows you to fill data into a range in any direction (down, right, left, and up). Choosing Fill Down in the submenu will copy the values in the cells on the top edge of the selected range into the rest of the range; choosing Fill Right will copy the values on the left-hand edge of the selected range into the rest of the range; and so on.

CREATING DATA SERIES

The AutoFill feature is one of Excel's "smart" features and can be used for more than just copying data into cell ranges. It can also be used to create data series across cell ranges, for example series of dates (Jan 1, Jan 2, Jan 3...), months (Jan, Feb, Mar...), days of the week (Mon, Tue, Wed...), and number series (1, 2, 3... or 5, 10, 15... etc). This can be time-saving when building certain types of worksheet.

1 CREATING A SERIES OF DAYS

• Into the Diary worksheet, type **Week Day** into cell B3, press Enter←, then type **Mon** (or **Monday**) into cell B4 and press Enter← again.

	A	B	C	D	E
1	Morning Appointments July 31 - August 4				
2	Director				
3		Week Day			
4	Mr Twizz	Mon			
5	Mr Twizz				
6	Mr Twizz				
7	Mr Twizz				

- Now select cell B4 again, put your mouse pointer over the fill handle, and drag the mouse pointer so that the gray AutoFill border surrounds the whole range B4 to B8.
- Release the mouse button. Instead of copying Mon into cells B5 to B8, AutoFill has filled these cells with the other days of the week (Tue, Wed, etc), which is what you want.

Don't want a series?

If you want to AutoFill a value like Jan, Tuesday, 9:00, or 12 Apr 2000, into a range of cells without producing a series, hold down the [Ctrl] key on the keyboard as you drag the fill handle. Doing this guarantees that you will get a simple fill instead of a series.

OTHER SERIES

You can also use AutoFill to produce series of months (Jan, Feb, Mar... , or January, February, March...), number series (for example, 1, 2, 3, 4... , or 10, 20, 30, 40...) and general series such as Period 1, Period 2, Period 3 etc. For all series except months, dates, days of the week, and hour series, you must type the first two items in the series that you want to create into adjacent cells, select them, and then drag the fill handle in order for the series to be incremented in the selected cells.

2 CREATING A SERIES OF DATES

• Type **Date** into cell C3 and 31 July 2000 into cell C4. Press [Enter ←].

• Select cell C4 again. Drag the fill handle to encompass the range C4 to C8.

• On releasing the mouse button, cells C5 to C8 fill with dates from 1 August to 4 August – again, exactly what you want.

	A	B	C	D	E	F
1	Morning Appointments July 31 - August 4					
2	Director					
3			Week Day	Date		
4	Mr Twizz	Mon	31 July 2000			
5	Mr Twizz	Tue				
6	Mr Twizz	Wed				
7	Mr Twizz	Thu				

	A	B	C	D	E	F
1	Morning Appointments July 31 - August 4					
2	Director					
3			Week Day	Date		
4	Mr Twizz	Mon	31-Jul-00			
5	Mr Twizz	Tue				
6	Mr Twizz	Wed				
7	Mr Twizz	Thu				
8	Mr Twizz	Fri				
9						
10				4-Aug-00		

3 CREATING A SERIES OF TIMES

Sometimes you need to provide AutoFill with the first two values in a series in order to end up with the series that you want.

• Type **9:00 AM** into cell D3 and **9:30 AM** into cell E3, then select both cells.

• Drag the fill handle across to G3 and release.

• The time series is extended into F3 and G3.

	A	B	C	D	E	F
1	Morning Appointments July 31 - August 4					
2	Director					
3			Week Day	Date	9:00 AM	9:30 AM
4	Mr Twizz	Mon	31-Jul-00			
5	Mr Twizz	Tue	1-Aug-00			
6	Mr Twizz	Wed	2-Aug-00			
7	Mr Twizz	Thu	3-Aug-00			

| = 9:00:00 AM |

B	C	D	E	F	G	H
pointments July 31 - August 4						
Week Day	Date	9:00 AM	9:30 AM			
Mon	31-Jul-00				10:30 AM	
Tue	1-Aug-00					
Wed	2-Aug-00					

| D3 | = 9:00:00 AM |

	A	B	C	D	E	F	G	H	I	J
1	Morning Appointments July 31 - August 4									
2	Director									
3			Week Day	Date	9:00 AM	9:30 AM	10:00 AM	10:30 AM		
4	Mr Twizz	Mon	31-Jul-00							
5	Mr Twizz	Tue	1-Aug-00							
6	Mr Twizz	Wed	2-Aug-00							
7	Mr Twizz	Thu	3-Aug-00							

COPYING AND PASTING

Copying and pasting is a technique used in many computer applications, not simply in Excel worksheets. All copy and paste operations work in the same way. You choose some data that you want to copy, and then use the Copy command. The original data stays where it is and the copy of the data is placed in a particular part of your computer's memory called the Clipboard. You then select where you would like the copied data to appear in your worksheet, and use the Paste command. The data is now copied from the Clipboard and placed in the chosen target area. You can repeat the Paste command to place the copied data over several different target areas if you wish. Copy and Paste commands can be carried out either via drop-down menus, toolbar buttons, or keyboard shortcuts.

1 COPYING A SINGLE CELL

In your Fantasy Ices Diary worksheet, you want to set up three appointments for a Ms. Black to meet with Mr. Twizz.
• Type **Ms. Black** into cell E4 and press (Enter↵).
• Select cell E4 again, and then choose Copy from the Edit menu.
• You will see a flashing outline appear around cell E4, indicating that its contents have been copied to the Clipboard.

	A	B	C	D	E	F
1	Morning Appointments July 31 - August 4					
2	Director					
3		Week Day	Date	09:00 AM	09:30 AM	10:00 AM	1(
4	Mr Twizz	Mon	31-Jul-00		Ms Black	
5	Mr Twizz	Tue	01-Aug-00			
6	Mr Twizz	Wed	02-Aug-00			
7	Mr Twizz	Thu	03-Aug-00			
8	Mr Twizz	Fri	04-Aug-00			
9						
10						

File Edit View Insert Format Tools Data Window Help

Undo Typing "Ms Black" in E4	Ctrl+Z
Repeat Auto Fill	Ctrl+Y
Cut	Ctrl+X
Copy	Ctrl+C
Paste	Ctrl+V
Paste Special...	
Paste as Hyperlink	

	A	B	C	D	E	F
1	Morning Appointments July 31 - August 4					
2	Director					
3		Week Day	Date	09:00 AM	09:30 AM	10:00 AM	1(
4	Mr Twizz	Mon	31-Jul-00		Ms Black	
5	Mr Twizz	Tue	01-Aug-00			
6	Mr Twizz	Wed	02-Aug-00			
7	Mr Twizz	Thu	03-Aug-00			

2 PASTING THE DATA

• Select cell E7 and then choose Paste from the Edit menu. Ms. Black is pasted into cell E7.

• Select cell F8 and repeat the Paste command. Press the [Esc] key to complete the copy/paste operation.

⌨ Undo Typing "Ms Black" in E4	Ctrl+Z				
↻ Can't Repeat	Ctrl+Y				
✂ Cut	Ctrl+X				
📋 Copy	Ctrl+C				
📋 Paste	Ctrl+V				
Paste Special...					
Paste as Hyperlink			9:30 AM	10:00 AM	
			Ms Black		
Fill	▶				
Clear	▶				

	F8	▼	= Ms Black				
	A	B	C	D	E	F	G
1	Morning Appointments July 31 - August 4						
2	Director						
3		Week Day	Date	9:00 AM	9:30 AM	10:00 AM	10:3
4	Mr Twizz	Mon	31-Jul-00		Ms Black		
5	Mr Twizz	Tue	1-Aug-00				
6	Mr Twizz	Wed	2-Aug-00				
7	Mr Twizz	Thu	3-Aug-00		Ms Black		
8	Mr Twizz	Fri	4-Aug-00			Ms Black	
9							

KEYBOARD SHORTCUTS

There are keyboard shortcuts for the Copy command and Paste command. To copy, hold down the [Ctrl] key and press C. To paste, hold down the [Ctrl] key and press V. These shortcuts are used universally across all PC applications, so they are worth remembering!

Want to move, not copy?

If you want to move data in a worksheet, that is, you want to place it in a new location without leaving a copy in the original location, this can be carried out by an operation called cut and paste 📋.

3 COPYING A BLOCK OF CELLS

You now want to copy and paste the whole of Mr. Twizz's diary to Mrs. Stick's part of the diary. When pasting a block of data, you need only select the top left-hand cell of the target area for the paste.

• Select the block B3 to G8 and click the Copy button on the Standard toolbar.

	B3	▼	= Week Day				
	A	B	C	D	E	F	G
1	Morning Appointments July 31 - August 4						
2	Director						
3		Week Day	Date	9:00 AM	9:30 AM	10:00 AM	10:3
4	Mr Twizz	Mon	31-Jul-00		Ms Black		
5	Mr Twizz	Tue	1-Aug-00				
6	Mr Twizz	Wed	2-Aug-00				
7	Mr Twizz	Thu	3-Aug-00		Ms Black		
8	Mr Twizz	Fri	4-Aug-00			Ms Black	
9							
10							
11	Mrs Stick						

4 PASTING THE COPIED BLOCK

• Select cell B10 – the top left-hand cell of your target area – and click the Paste button on the Standard toolbar.

• The copied data is pasted over the range B10 to G15. Your "fantasyices.xls" workbook can now be saved.

Pasted cells

MULTIPLE PASTES

To carry out multiple pastes after a Copy command, hold down the [Ctrl] key and then select, one by one, the various target cells for your pastes. You then simply choose Paste from the Edit menu. Alternatively, click the Paste button on the Standard toolbar.

Pasting Care

When copying and pasting a block of cells, if you try to select the whole target area for the paste, but get the size wrong, Excel will come up with an error message, saying that the Copy and Paste areas don't match. It's generally better to select just the top left-hand cell of the target area. But always be careful when pasting blocks of cells – there is a risk of overpasting existing data in the worksheet, and you get no warning if this is about to happen.

COPYING BY DRAG AND DROP

Drag and Drop is another very useful method for copying data from one cell or block of cells to another part of the worksheet. It is a quick method, because it is performed by dragging with the mouse rather than by choosing menu commands or toolbar buttons. However, it does require a little practice.

1 COPYING A SINGLE CELL

In the Diary sheet of the "fantasyices.xls" workbook, you can practice some drags and drops after filling in some more dates for the directors of Fantasy Ices.

● Type **Dr. Green** into cell D6. Position your mouse pointer over the bottom border of cell D6, and it turns into an arrow. Hold down the mouse button.

● Hold down the [Ctrl] key. A + sign appears next to the mouse pointer.

●Drag the mouse so that the mouse pointer moves down the worksheet. A gray rectangular outline, the same size as a cell, moves down the screen following the mouse pointer and the + sign. A yellow label with a cell address (like D8) on it also travels with the mouse pointer. This continually updates and indicates which cell the gray outline has reached.

	A	B	C	D	E
1	Morning Appointments July 31 - August 4				
2	Director				
3		Week Day	Date	9:00 AM	9:30 AM
4	Mr Twizz	Mon	31-Jul-00		Ms Black
5	Mr Twizz	Tue	1-Aug-00		
6	Mr Twizz	Wed	2-Aug-00	Dr Green	
7	Mr Twizz	Thu	3-Aug-00		Ms Black
8	Mr Twizz	Fri	4-Aug-00		

	A	B	C	D	E
1	Morning Appointments July 31 - August 4				
2	Director				
3		Week Day	Date	9:00 AM	9:30 AM
4	Mr Twizz	Mon	31-Jul-00		Ms Black
5	Mr Twizz	Tue	1-Aug-00		
6	Mr Twizz	Wed	2-Aug-00	Dr Green	
7	Mr Twizz	Thu	3-Aug-00		Ms Black
8	Mr Twizz	Fri	4-Aug-00		

	A	B	C	D	E
1	Morning Appointments July 31 - August 4				
2	Director				
3		Week Day	Date	09:00 AM	09:30 AM
4	Mr Twizz	Mon	31-Jul-00		Ms Black
5	Mr Twizz	Tue	01-Aug-00		
6	Mr Twizz	Wed	02-Aug-00	Dr Green	
7	Mr Twizz	Thu	03-Aug-00		Ms Black
8	Mr Twizz	Fri	04-Aug-00		
9					
10		Week Day	Date	09:00 AM	09:30 AM

• Drag until the gray outline reaches cell D13. Now for the "drop." Release the mouse button and finally the [Ctrl] key. Dr. Green is copied to cell D13.

	A	B	C	D	E	F
11	Mrs Stick	Mon	31-Jul-00		Ms Black	
12	Mrs Stick	Tue	1-Aug-00			
13	Mrs Stick	Wed	2-Aug-00	Dr Green		
14	Mrs Stick	Thu	3-Aug-00		Ms Black	
15	Mrs Stick	Fri	4-Aug-00			Ms Black
16						

2 COPYING A BLOCK OF CELLS

You can drag and drop blocks of cells just as easily as single cells. Try this simple exercise.

• Select the range D4 to E6, and move the mouse pointer over the bottom border of the selection until you see the pointer turn into an arrow.

	A	B	C	D	E	F
1	Morning Appointments July 31 - August 4					
2	Director					
3		Week Day	Date	09:00 AM	09:30 AM	10:00 AM	1(
4	Mr Twizz	Mon	31-Jul-00		Ms Black	
5	Mr Twizz	Tue	01-Aug-00			
6	Mr Twizz	Wed	02-Aug-00	Dr Green		
7	Mr Twizz	Thu	03-Aug-00		Ms Black	

• Hold down the mouse button and the [Ctrl] key, and drag the mouse to the right until the gray rectangular outline surrounds the range F4 to G6. Then release the mouse button and [Ctrl] key.

	A	B	C	D	E	F
1	Morning Appointments July 31 - August 4					
2	Director					
3		Week Day	Date	09:00 AM	09:30 AM	10:00 AM	1(
4	Mr Twizz	Mon	31-Jul-00		Ms Black	
5	Mr Twizz	Tue	01-Aug-00			
6	Mr Twizz	Wed	02-Aug-00	Dr Green		
7	Mr Twizz	Thu	03-Aug-00		Ms Black	

• The dragged range gets pasted into F4 to G6.

B	C	D	E	F	G	H
ppointments July 31 - August 4						
Week Day	Date	09:00 AM	09:30 AM	10:00 AM	10:30 AM	
Mon	31-Jul-00		Ms Black		Ms Black	
ue	01-Aug-00					
Wed	02-Aug-00	Dr Green		Dr Green		
hu	03-Aug-00		Ms Black			

Control to Copy

If you forget to hold down the [Ctrl] key during a drag and drop operation, you will find that you move the dragged data instead of copying it.

WHEN TO DRAG AND DROP

Drag and drop is just one way of copying data. The drag and drop technique in Excel is most useful for copying data over short distances on a worksheet. For copying data over longer distances, or from one worksheet to another, use the Copy and Paste technique. For copying from a cell to an adjacent cell (or cells), it is better to use Fill or AutoFill.

INSERTING NEW COLUMNS, ROWS, AND CELLS

It is in the nature of worksheets for them to grow and evolve over time, and it is common to extend them by adding new columns, rows, or individual cells as the need arises. When you do this, you have to shift some of the existing cells, together with their contents, to the right or further down in the worksheet in order to create room for the new cells. This usually causes no problems, although it does require some thought, especially when inserting individual cells or groups of cells.

1 INSERTING A COLUMN

The company directors of Fantasy Ices want to make some 8:30 appointments to meet up with each other. This requires the creation of a new column in the Diary worksheet.
- Select column D by clicking on the column D header button. This is where you want the new column to appear.
- Choose Columns from the Insert menu.

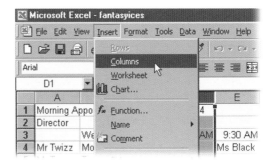

• A new blank column is inserted and the original contents of column D, and the contents of columns to the right of column D, are all automatically shifted one column to the right.

• Now type **8:30 AM** into cell D3 and copy this time to cell D10.

• Add some appropriate appointments to column D.

	A	B	C	D	E
	D1		=		
1	Morning Appointments July 31 - August 4				
2	Director				
3		Week Day	Date		9:00 AM
4	Mr Twizz	Mon	31-Jul-00		
5	Mr Twizz	Tue	1-Aug-00		
6	Mr Twizz	Wed	2-Aug-00		Dr Green
7	Mr Twizz	Thu	3-Aug-00		
8	Mr Twizz	Fri	4-Aug-00		

	A	B	C	D	E
6	Mr Twizz	Wed	2-Aug-00	Mrs Stick	Dr Green
7	Mr Twizz	Thu	3-Aug-00	Mrs Stick	
8	Mr Twizz	Fri	4-Aug-00		
9					
10		Week Day	Date	8:30 AM	9:00 AM
11	Mrs Stick	Mon	31-Jul-00		
12	Mrs Stick	Tue	1-Aug-00		
13	Mrs Stick	Wed	2-Aug-00	Mr Twizz	Dr Green

	A	B	C	D	E
6	Mr Twizz	Wed	2-Aug-00		Dr Green
7	Mr Twizz	Thu	3-Aug-00		
8	Mr Twizz	Fri	4-Aug-00		
9					
10		Week Day	Date	8:30 AM	9:00 AM
11	Mrs Stick	Mon	31-Jul-00		
12	Mrs Stick	Tue	1-Aug-00		
13	Mrs Stick	Wed	2-Aug-00		Dr Green
14	Mrs Stick	Thu	3-Aug-00		
15	Mrs Stick	Fri	4-Aug-00		
16					

CONTEXT SENSITIVE MENUS

Note that Excel's drop-down menus are context-sensitive. After you have selected a column in a worksheet, the Insert Rows command is not a feasible command, and so it is grayed out on the Insert menu. When a row or rows is selected, the Insert Columns command is similarly grayed out.

WHAT SHIFTS WHERE?

Remember that when you choose to insert a new column or columns, they are inserted at the left-hand side of the column(s) that you selected on the worksheet before choosing Insert Columns. When you insert some new row(s) they are inserted above the row(s) that you selected on the worksheet. There is no choice as to the direction in which columns or rows get shifted – this choice only appears when you insert one or more cells.

2 INSERTING TWO ROWS

Mr. Twizz wants to make some Saturday and Sunday appointments. This means adding two more rows to the worksheet.

• Select rows 9 and 10. This is where you want the new rows to appear.

• Choose Rows from the Insert menu.

• New blank rows are inserted and the original contents of rows 9, 10, 11 etc, are all automatically shifted two rows down.

• Select the range A8 to C8 and AutoFill these cells down to A10-C10. Enter some weekend appointments for Mr. Twizz by typing **Mr. Brown** into cells E9 and F10.

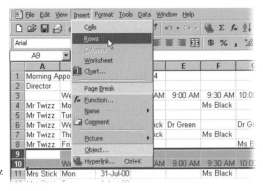

AutoFilled cells

3 INSERTING A FEW CELLS

Mr. Twizz wants to make some extra appointments for 9:15, but Mrs. Stick doesn't need to. You want to add some individual cells, but not a whole row or column, to Mr. Twizz's part of the worksheet.

- Select the range F3-F10.
- Choose Cells from the Insert menu.

- The Insert dialog box appears. To create room for your new cells, you have the choice of shifting the existing range F3-F10 (and all cells to the right) further to the right; or to shift F3-F10 (and all cells below) down. You want to shift the existing cells to the right, so just click on OK.

- Now type **9:15 AM** into cell F3, and fill in some 9:15 appointments with Ms. Orange in cells F6 and F7 for Mr. Twizz. Save your "fantasyices.xls" workbook.

COPYING AND INSERTING

Copying and inserting consists of a combination of an Insert operation and a Copy/Paste operation. On occasions you will want to make a copy of a cell or a whole range of cells and place this copy on the worksheet but without pasting over and losing existing contents. So you need to create some extra room in the worksheet to take the copy. You could create this extra space with an Insert command, and then do a Copy/Paste. However, a Copy/Insert operation is quicker as it achieves the same result with a smaller number of actions.

1 COPY/INSERT IN SEVERAL ROWS

A new Director, Mr. Bloggs, has joined Fantasy Ices. He needs a space for his own appointments in the Diary sheet of "fantasyices.xls," and his first appointments will be the same as those of Mr. Twizz.

	A	B	C	D	E	F
1	Morning Appointments July 31 - August 4					
2	Director					
3		Week Day	Date	8:30 AM	9:00 AM	9:15 AM	9:
4	Mr Twizz	Mon	31-Jul-00				Ms
5	Mr Twizz	Tue	1-Aug-00				
6	Mr Twizz	Wed	2-Aug-00	Mrs Stick	Dr Green	Ms Orange	
7	Mr Twizz	Thu	3-Aug-00	Mrs Stick		Ms Orange	Ms
8	Mr Twizz	Fri	4-Aug-00				
9	Mr Twizz	Sat	5-Aug-00		Mr Brown		
10	Mr Twizz	Sun	6-Aug-00				Mr
11							

• Select the rows you want to copy and insert – in this case, rows 3 to 11. Then click on the Copy button.

• Select a row where you would like the copied data to be inserted – in this case row 12.

	A	B	C	D	E	F
10	Mr Twizz	Sun	6-Aug-00				Mr
11							
12		Week Day	Date	8:30 AM	9:00 AM	9:30 AM	10:
13	Mrs Stick	Mon	31-Jul-00			Ms Black	
14	Mrs Stick	Tue	1-Aug-00				

• Choose Copied Cells from the Insert menu. The copied data is inserted into the worksheet.

File Edit View Insert Format Tools Data Window Help
Copied Cells
Rows

• Now type **Mr. Bloggs** into cell A13 and AutoFill down to cell A19. Mr. Bloggs now has his own section of the appointments diary.

	A	B	C	D	E	F
12		Week Day	Date	8:30 AM	9:00 AM	9:15 AM	9:
13	Mr Bloggs	Mon	31-Jul-00				Ms
14	Mr Bloggs	Tue	1-Aug-00				
15	Mr Bloggs	Wed	2-Aug-00	Mrs Stick	Dr Green	Ms Orange	
16	Mr Bloggs	Thu	3-Aug-00	Mrs Stick		Ms Orange	Ms
17	Mr Bloggs	Fri	4-Aug-00				
18	Mr Bloggs	Sat	5-Aug-00		Mr Brown		
19	Mr Bloggs	Sun	6-Aug-00				Mr
20							

COPY, DRAG, AND INSERT!

It is possible to copy, drag, and insert cells through a technique similar to copy, drag, and drop. To copy, drag, and insert, select the cell or cells to copy, and then hold down both Ctrl and

⇧ Shift. Drag your selection to the insert/paste target area. You will see a gray outline shape follow the mouse pointer. If you want existing cells in the worksheet to move right when the insert happens,

place this gray outline to the left of the target area. If you want existing cells to move down, place the gray outline above the target area. Then release the mouse button and both keyboard keys.

2 COPY/INSERT A SINGLE CELL

At the other extreme, try copy/inserting a single cell. Dr. Green needs an extra appointment with Mr. Twizz at 9:30 AM on Thursday. This time slot is already taken up by Ms. Black. No matter – with a copy/insert, Dr. Green can have the 9:30 AM time slot and the appointment with Ms. Black can be put back by half an hour.

● Select cell E6 and click on the Copy button.

● Click on cell G7 (the intended time slot) and choose Copied Cells from the Insert menu.

● When the Insert Paste dialog appears, choose Shift cells right and click on OK.

● Dr. Green gets her 9:30 AM appointment with Mr. Twizz and Ms. Black's appointment is put back to 10:00 AM.

EDITING WORKSHEETS

This chapter is about editing existing worksheets. You can change the contents of cells, check spellings, move cells, add comments, remove cell contents, or delete the cells altogether.

CHANGING CELL CONTENTS

You can change the contents of a cell in its entirety or only part of the contents. For example, you can shorten a text label, or change the month but keep the original day. There is a single straightforward method for changing all of a cell's contents, and there are two distinct methods for making partial changes. These two methods are called "in-cell editing", and "editing in the formula bar." The examples given below are applied to the Sales worksheet of "fantasyices.xls."

1 CHANGING A TEXT LABEL

The directors of Fantasy Ices have decided to relaunch Twizzlesticks under a new name.

• Select cell A3 – the cell that contains the Twizzlesticks label.

• Type the new name – **Kooltwists**. Press [Enter ↵].
Note that the new label takes on the same format as the old label – when you change a cell's contents, it retains its format.

2 ALTERING FORMULA VALUES

There's an update required to the sales data for orange sorbets – that is, to the value held in cell B5.

• Select cell B5 and revise the number for the sales of boxes of orange sorbets.

• Press [Enter←]. Note that when you confirm the change to cell B5, the value in cell D5 (the sales revenue from orange sorbets) and D7 (total revenue) also change. This makes sense, but how has it happened?

• Click on cell D5 and look in the Formula bar. When there is a formula in the active cell, it shows in the Formula bar. Cell D5 contains the formula: =**B5*C5**. When you change any cell value referenced by a formula, Excel automatically updates the value in the cell containing that formula. Because you changed B5, Excel has automatically updated D5, which contains a formula referencing B5.

• Click on cell D7. It contains the formula: =**SUM(D3:D6)**. Because cell D5 (which is contained in the referenced range D3:D6) changed, the value in D7 updated as well.

	B5	▾	X √ =	145	
	A	B	C		D
1					
2	Product	Sales (boxes)	Price ($)		Sales Revenue
3	Kooltwists	3467	$	6.25	$ 21,668.75
4	Chokky bars	893	$	0.74	$ 660.82
5	Orange sorbet	145	$	21.33	$ 2,090.34
6	Raspberry surprise	345	$	12.75	$ 4,398.75
7			Total Revenue		$ 28,818.66
8					

	B6	▾	=	345	
	A	B	C		D
1					
2	Product	Sales (boxes)	Price ($)		Sales Revenue
3	Kooltwists	3467	$	6.25	$ 21,668.75
4	Chokky bars	893	$	0.74	$ 660.82
5	Orange sorbet	145	$	21.33	$ 3,092.85
6	Raspberry surprise	345	$	12.75	$ 4,398.75
7			Total Revenue		$ 29,821.17
8					
9					
10		Last Updated			

	D5	▾	=	=B5*C5	
	A	B	C		D
1					
2	Product	Sales (boxes)	Price ($)		Sales Revenue
3	Kooltwists	3467	$	6.25	$ 21,668.75
4	Chokky bars	893	$	0.74	$ 660.82
5	Orange sorbet	145	$	21.33	$ 3,092.85
6	Raspberry surprise	345	$	12.75	$ 4,398.75
7			Total Revenue		$ 29,821.17
8					
9					
10		Last Updated			

	D7	▾	=	=SUM(D3:D6)	
	A	B	C		D
1					
2	Product	Sales (boxes)	Price ($)		Sales Revenue
3	Kooltwists	3467	$	6.25	$ 21,668.75
4	Chokky bars	893	$	0.74	$ 660.82
5	Orange sorbet	145	$	21.33	$ 3,092.85
6	Raspberry surprise	345	$	12.75	$ 4,398.75
7			Total Revenue		$ 29,821.17
8					
9					
10		Last Updated			

3 IN-CELL EDITING OF TEXT LABELS

Chokky bars are getting a name-change to plain "Chocolate bars." You can make this change by means of an in-cell edit.

• Double-click in the middle of cell A4. This prepares the cell for in-cell editing. The cell is ready to edit if you see an insertion point (small vertical bar) flashing between two letters in the cell.

• Click the mouse pointer before the first **k** in **Chokky**, then hold down the mouse button and drag the mouse to the right to highlight the string of letters **kky**. This is the part of the label that you want to replace. Now release the mouse button.

• Type **clate** and press Enter⏎ to leave **Choclate bars** (don't worry that you've introduced a deliberate spelling mistake! – you'll see why shortly).

• Now change **Raspberry surprise** to **Raspberry sundar** (again don't worry about the spelling mistake).

Arial		10		**B**	*I*	U

A4	▾	✕ ✓	=	Chokky bars

	A	B	C	
1				
2	Product	Sales (boxes)	Price ($)	Sal
3	Kooltwists	3467	$ 6.25	$
4	Chokky bars	893	$ 0.74	$
5	Orange sorbet	145	$ 21.33	$
6	Raspberry surprise	345	$ 12.75	$

Arial		10		**B**	*I*	U

	▾	✕ ✓	=	Chokky bars

	A	B	C	
1				
2	Product	Sales (boxes)	Price ($)	Sal
3	Kooltwists	3467	$ 6.25	$
4	Chokky bars	893	$ 0.74	$
5	Orange sorbet	145	$ 21.33	$
6	Raspberry surprise	345	$ 12.75	$

A4	▾	✕ ✓	=	Choclate bars

	A	B	C	
1				
2	Product	Sales (boxes)	Price ($)	Sal
3	Kooltwists	3467	$ 6.25	$
4	Choclate bars	893	$ 0.74	$
5	Orange sorbet	145	$ 21.33	$
6	Raspberry surprise	345	$ 12.75	$

A6	▾	✕ ✓	=	Raspberry sundar

	A	B	C	
1				
2	Product	Sales (boxes)	Price ($)	Sal
3	Kooltwists	3467	$ 6.25	$
4	Choclate bars	893	$ 0.74	$
5	Orange sorbet	145	$ 21.33	$
6	Raspberry sundar		$ 12.75	$
7			Total Revenue	$

4 EDITING IN THE FORMULA BAR

• Now click on cell C11, which contains the date 7 June 2000. You want to change this date to 15 August 2000.

• Place your mouse pointer in the Formula bar and you will see that it changes into an I-shaped cursor.

• Click to the right of the figure **7**, press down on the mouse button, and drag the pointer to the left to highlight the string of characters **6/7**. This is the part that you want to change. Now release the mouse button.

• Type **8/15** and finally press [Enter←].

On Second Thoughts...

If, while making a change to a cell, you decide not to make the change after all, you can abort the change by pressing the [Esc] key.

	A	B	C	D
1				
2	Product	Sales (boxes)	Price ($)	Sales Revenue
3	Kooltwists	3467	$ 6.25	$ 21,668.75
4	Choclate bars	893	$ 0.74	$ 660.82
5	Orange sorbet	145	$ 21.33	$ 3,092.85
6	Raspberry sundar	345	$ 12.75	$ 4,398.75
7			Total Revenue	$ 29,821.17
8				
9				
10		Last Updated		
11		Date	7-Jun-00	

Arial		10	B I U	三 三 三
C11		=	6/7/2000	

	A	B		Sal
1				
2	Product	Sales (boxes)	Price ($)	
3	Kooltwists	3467	$ 6.25	$
4	Choclate bars	893	$ 0.74	$
5	Orange sorbet	145	$ 21.33	$
6	Raspberry sundar	345	$ 12.75	$

Arial		10	B I U	三 三 三
C11	X ✓	=	6/7/2000	

	A	B	C
1			
2	Product	Sales (boxes)	Price ($)	Sal
3	Kooltwists	3467	$ 6.25	$
4	Choclate bars	893	$ 0.74	$

Arial		10	B I U	三 三 三
C11	X ✓	=	8/15/2000	

	A	B	C
1			
2	Product	Sales (boxes)	Price ($)	Sal
3	Kooltwists	3467	$ 6.25	$
4	Choclate bars	893	$ 0.74	$
5	Orange sorbet	145	$ 21.33	$
6	Raspberry sundar	345	$ 12.75	$
7			Total Revenue	$

CHECKING SPELLING

Excel provides a tool for checking the spelling of the text in your worksheets. The Spelling tool works by checking the spelling of each word against a built-in dictionary. When the Spelling tool finds a mistake, it offers you the choice of correcting the error or not, and in most cases will suggest the correct spelling. You have the opportunity to add specialist words, which Excel doesn't recognize, to your own custom dictionary so that the Spelling tool doesn't query them again.

1 STARTING THE SPELLING TOOL

The Spelling tool checks each word in each cell, row by row, starting from the active cell. Unless a range of cells is selected when you check spelling, the tool checks the entire work-sheet, including both cell values and comments ⬚.
• To check the whole worksheet, select its top left-hand cell. In this case, select cell A1 of the Sales worksheets in "fantasyices.xls." Click the Spelling button on the Standard toolbar.

Habitual Misspeller

If there is a particular word that you habitually mistype or misspell, try putting it on an AutoCorrect list. This feature automatically corrects specified misspellings whenever you make them. To add to the AutoCorrect list, choose AutoCorrect from the Tools menu. Type your habitual misspell in the Replace: box, then the correct spelling in the With box, and click on OK.

DON'T EXPECT THE IMPOSSIBLE

Remember that the Spelling tool cannot pick up a typing error if the mistype gives rise to another, correctly spelled, word. For example, if you mistype "product" as "produce," the Spelling tool will not see this as an error! So you should do a visual check after using the Spelling tool.

---

62   Adding and Editing Comments

2 ADDING TO YOUR DICTIONARY

• The Spelling tool displays the Spelling dialog box when a word is found that it doesn't recognize. If you want to add this word to your own custom dictionary so that it is not queried again, check that CUSTOM.DIC appears in the Add words to: box, then click on the Add button.

3 SPELLING TOOL SUGGESTIONS

• When the Spelling tool comes across **Choclate**, it suggests that this should be changed to **Chocolate**. You agree, so click on the Change button.

4 ACCEPTING A SPELLING

• When the Spelling tool comes across **sundar**, it provides various spelling suggestions of what you meant to type. In this case, click on **sundae** in the Suggestions box, and then click on the Change button.

• Once the Spelling tool has checked the entire sheet for misspellings, it comes up with a task completion message. Just click on OK.

MOVING AND SWAPPING DATA

Moving data is similar to copying data, except that you leave no copy of the data behind in its original location. You can move data by cut and paste, or by drag and drop. These techniques are similar to copy and paste and copying by drag and drop. You can also carry out cut/inserts, which are similar to copy/inserts; but again they leave no copy of your original data on the worksheet.

MOVING BY CUT AND PASTE

For a cut and paste, you first select a cell or cells that you want to move and then carry out a Cut command. You then choose a target area for the move and carry out a Paste command.
• In the Diary Sheet of your "fantasyices.xls" workbook, select cell E6 (Dr. Green), and then click the Cut button on the Standard toolbar.
• An outline flashes around cell E6. Select cell E8 and click on the Paste button.

Copying
and Pasting

Copying by
Drag and Drop

50 Copying and
Inserting

• Dr. Green appears in cell E8 and disappears from E6. The data has moved from E6 to E8.

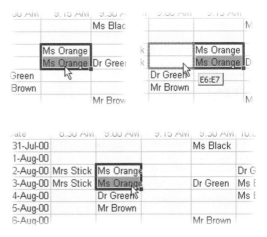

MOVING BY DRAG AND DROP

Moving by drag and drop is identical to copying by drag and drop, except that you don't need to hold down the Ctrl key.

• Select cells F6 and F7 (which both contain Ms. Orange). Place the mouse pointer over the bottom border of F7 and see that it turns into an arrow.

• Hold down the mouse button and drag the mouse to the left. Once you have positioned the gray outline over cells E6 and E7, release the mouse button.

• The data in cells F6 and F7 moves across.

SWAPPING ROWS AND COLUMNS

To swap two adjacent columns, click the right-hand column and click on the Cut button. Now click the left-hand column and choose Cut Cells from the Insert menu. To swap two adjacent rows, select and cut the lower row, then select the upper row and choose Cut Cells from the Insert menu.

CUTTING AND INSERTING

When you cut and insert, the cut data is removed from one part of the worksheet and placed into new cell(s) inserted elsewhere in the worksheet. Normally, you have to specify where existing cells should move to accommodate the new cells.

• Select cell G4 (Ms. Black). Click on the Cut button.

• Select cell E9 and choose Cut Cells from the Insert menu on the Menu bar.

• In the Insert Paste dialog box, choose Shift cells right.

• Ms. Black moves from cell G4 to cell E9. Other cells in row 9 are shifted to the right to accommodate the new insertion.

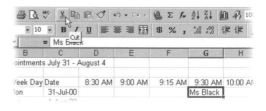

How Does Moving Affect Formulas?

Special repercussions arise from moving (or copying) formulas, cells containing formulas, or cells referenced by formulas within a worksheet. For full details, you will need to consult a separate *Essential DK Computers* guide on Excel formulas. However, Excel generally arranges for formulas to continue working wherever they are moved, or wherever data referenced by the formulas is moved.

KEYBOARD SHORTCUT

There is a quick keyboard shortcut for the Cut command. Hold down the Ctrl key and then press the x key. Remember that Ctrl plus C can be used for the Copy command, and Ctrl plus v for the Paste command.

	A	B	C	D	E	F
1	Morning Appointments July 31 - August 4					
2	Director					
3		Week Day	Date	08:30 AM	09:00 AM	09:15 AM	09:3
4	Mr Twizz	Mon	31-Jul-00			
5	Mr Twizz	Tue	01-Aug-00			
6	Mr Twizz	Wed	02-Aug-00	Mrs Stick	Ms Orange	
7	Mr Twizz	Thu	03-Aug-00	Mrs Stick	Ms Orange		Dr G
8	Mr Twizz	Fri	04-Aug-00		Dr Green	
9	Mr Twizz	Sat	05-Aug-00		Ms Black	Mr Brown
10	Mr Twizz	Sun	06-Aug-00				Mr E

SWAPPING CELLS BY CUTTING AND INSERTING

If you cut some data and then attempt to insert it elsewhere in the same row or column, Excel manages the operation differently from other cut/insert operations. Instead of creating new cells, it moves the actual cells containing the data, and you are given no choice as to the direction in which other cells should be shifted. The positions of the moved and displaced cells are swapped, which is usually what you want to happen.

• In your Sales worksheet, you want to swap the data in rows 5 (Orange sorbet) and 4 (Chocolate bars). First select the range of cells A5 to D5, and click on the Cut button.

• Now select cells A4 to D4 and choose Cut Cells from the Insert menu.

• The cells that were previously A5 to D5 are moved to A4 to D4, and the cells that were previously A4 to D4 automatically drop down to occupy A5 to D5.

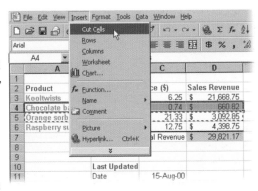

ADDING AND EDITING COMMENTS

So far, you have seen that a cell can contain text, numerical values, and formulas. A cell also has a format associated with it and every cell has a name. A further property that can be associated with a cell is a comment. This is like a note attached to the cell. You can easily add comments to cells and they can be displayed, changed, edited, or deleted at any time in the future.

1 ADDING A COMMENT

• Select a cell to which you would like to add a comment. For this example, select cell A15 in the Sales sheet of the "fantasyices.xls" workbook. Choose Comment from the Insert menu.

• A pale-yellow comment box appears, joined by a short arrow to the cell it refers to. At the top of the box, Microsoft Excel automatically inserts the name of the licensed user, which it assumes is the "commentator." Below this is a flashing insertion point.

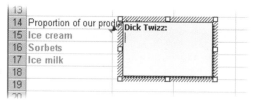

SHORTCUT MENUS

Note that the context-sensitive shortcut menu that appears when you right-click a cell contains several commonly used actions, including Copy, Paste, and Insert. Also Cut and Clear Contents as well as Insert Comment or Edit Comment.

58 Moving by cut and paste

66 Clearing cell contents

- Type your comment.
- If you are someone different from the recorded licensed user and you wish to register this, double-click on the person's name to highlight it. Then type your own name in its place.
- To close the comment, click on a blank cell outside the comment box.

2 DISPLAY AND EDIT COMMENTS

Cells with comments attached have a small red triangle at their top right-hand corners.

- Move the mouse pointer over cell A15, and the comment is displayed automatically.
- To edit the comment, move the mouse pointer over the cell and click the right mouse button. A shortcut menu appears. Choose Edit Comment from the shortcut menu.
- You can now type in some more text or edit the existing text.

3 RESIZING A COMMENT BOX

If the amount of text in a comment box becomes too long for the box, you can resize the box.

• Place your mouse pointer over the bottom right-hand corner of the comment attached to cell A15. You will see it turn into a double-headed arrow.

• Hold down the left mouse button and drag the corner of the comment box to resize it. You will see an outline preview of the new box size.

• Release the mouse button once you are happy with the new size of the box.

Double-headed arrow

Proportion of our prod
Ice cream
Sorbets
Ice milk

Susan Stick:
I think we can classify the chocolate bars as ice cream, for now at least. Even though they

---

LOTS OF COMMENTS

To display all comments on a worksheet at the same time, choose Options from the Tools menu and click on the View tab at the top of the dialog box. Choose Comment & indicator, and then click on OK. Change the option back to Comment indicator only to hide comments.

Proportion of our prod
Ice cream
Sorbets
Ice milk

Susan Stick:
I think we can classify the chocolate bars as ice cream, for now at least. Even though they contain only about 35 percent ice cream, the rest is toffee and chocolate.

Sheet1 / Sheet2 / Sheet3 /

CLEARING CELLS

Occasionally you'll want to remove some worksheet data. You can either clear or delete relevant cells. Of these, clearing is the less drastic maneuver. When you clear a cell, you remove some (or all) of the items associated with the cell without removing the cell itself. You have to choose whether you want to remove the cell's contents, its format, comments attached to the cell, or all of these at once.

1 CLEARING A FORMAT

You can clear the format from a cell without changing its contents (values or formulas it contains). The cell then reverts to a "general" format – the standard format that all cells have before they are given any special format.

• In the Sales worksheet, choose cell B10, which reads "Last Updated."
• Choose Clear from the Edit menu, and Formats from the submenu.
• Cell B10 reverts to a standard format.

Clearing a Comment

To clear a comment (but not content or format) from a cell, right-click the cell and choose Delete Comment from the pop-up menu.

2 CLEARING CELL CONTENTS

It is common practice to clear cell contents, but you must remember that clearing contents alone does not remove formats and comments.

- Select cells A15 and B15 in the Sales worksheet.

- With the mouse pointer over cell B15, click the right mouse button and a pop-up shortcut menu appears. Choose Clear Contents.

- The cells' contents have been removed, but the little red triangle indicates that there is still a comment attached to cell A15.

- Cell A15 has also retained its special format. Type **Ice cream** back into the cell and the continuing presence of both the comment and special format becomes apparent.

CLEARING BY FILLING

An alternative method for clearing cells is to use the Fill Handle to duplicate empty, blank cells over the area you wish to clear. This method clears the contents and formats but not the comments.

3 CLEARING ALL FROM CELLS

If you want to clear out a
cell completely, returning it
to a pristine state, use the
Clear All command.
• Select the range A14 to
B17 in the Sales worksheet.
• Choose Clear from the
Edit menu and then choose
All from the submenu.
• Everything – contents,
formats, and comments –
has now been removed.

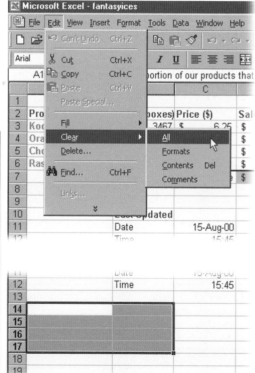

CLEARING WITH THE KEYBOARD

You can clear contents
(not formats and
comments) from a cell,
or a range of cells, by
selecting the cell(s) and
then hitting the ← Bksp
or Del. Never try to
clear a cell by typing a
space into it (using the
keyboard spacebar). The
cell may look empty, but
it actually contains a
space character that
could cause problems
later on.

DELETING COLUMNS, ROWS, AND CELLS

Deleting columns, rows, and cells means removing the actual cells from the worksheet and not just the cell contents. Just as nature abhors a vacuum, similarly Excel cannot tolerate "holes" in worksheets. So when cells, rows, or columns are deleted, other cells in the worksheet have to be shifted in order to plug the gap. Deletions are thus the diametric opposite of insertions ◁.

1 DELETING A COLUMN

Try practicing some deletions on the Diary worksheet you have created in the "fantasyices.xls" workbook.

• Mr. Twizz and Mrs. Stick decide they don't want to meet up for any 8:30 appointments after all. Select column D, and then choose Delete from the Edit menu.

• Column D is deleted, and all columns to the right of column D shift one column to the left.

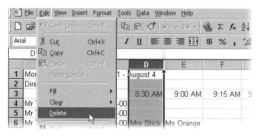

2 DELETING A FEW ROWS

Mr Bloggs leaves, so he no longer requires space in the Diary worksheet.

• Select rows 12 to 20, click on the right mouse button, and choose Delete from the pop-up menu.

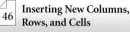

46 Inserting New Columns, Rows, and Cells

• Rows 12 to 20 disappear, and the rows below row 20 move up to fill the gap that the deletion created.

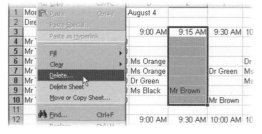

3 DELETING SOME CELLS

• Mr. Twizz decides to cancel his 9:15 appointments. Select cells E3 to E10, and then choose Delete from the Edit menu.

• A dialog box appears asking whether you want to shift cells left or shift cells up. Choose Shift cells left and click on OK.

• Cells E3 to E10 are removed, and cells to the right are shifted left.

SURE YOU WANT TO DELETE?

Before deleting cells, ask yourself whether you really just want to clear them . Deleting cells removes the cells from the worksheet and moves other worksheet cells. If all you want to do is to "blank out" some cells, use the Clear command instead.

GLOSSARY

ACTIVE CELL
The cell with the thick, black border around it on a worksheet or, in a selected block of cells, the white cell. When you type, the characters appear in the active cell as well as in the Formula bar above the worksheet.

AUTOFILL
AutoFill is used to copy a cell's contents and format into a block of adjacent cells, or to create a data series by dragging the fill handle.

COMMENT
A comment is a note that is attached to a particular cell and usually contains text.

CELL ADDRESS
The location of a cell as defined by the column and row it is in – for example, C5 or G9.

CELL CONTENTS
The text, numerical value, or formula that you have entered into a cell. You can check the contents of a cell by selecting it and looking in the Formula bar. If a cell contains a formula, then what appears in the cell on screen is different from what the cell contains. What appears on screen is the value of the cell that has been calculated by the formula it contains, and which is shown in the Formula bar.

CELL VALUE
What you see in a cell on screen is the cell's value. A value can be numerical, such as

a number or a date, or a text value. There is a distinction between constant values, which are never affected when the values of other cells change; and variable values, which are calculated by formulas that use the values of other cells. Variable values change when the value of cells elsewhere in the worksheet change. An empty cell has a value of 0.

FILL
Copying a cell's contents and formatting it into a block of adjacent cells.

FILL HANDLE
A small dark square at the bottom right of a selected cell or range of cells. It can be dragged using the mouse to carry out an AutoFill.

FORMAT
An aspect of the way a cell looks or behaves. Such aspects include the cell's size and color; any borders it may have; the typeface, size, and color used for any characters displayed in a cell; the alignment of those characters; and the way numbers are displayed (for example, with or without a decimal point). A collection of formats is called a style.

FORMULA
An expression entered into a cell that calculates the value of that cell from a combination of constants, arithmetic operators, and (often) the values of other cells in the worksheet.

All formulas start with the "=" character. A formula can also contain a function.

FORMULA BAR
The white bar above the worksheet that always shows the contents of the active cell.

FUNCTION
A defined operation or set of operations that can be performed on one or more selected cell values, cell addresses, or other data. Functions are incorporated into formulas. Excel functions include the function SUM, which returns the result of adding a defined range of values together.

NUMERICAL VALUE
A number, date, time, percentage, or monetary amount.

RANGE
A block of cells.

SELECTED CELLS / SELECTION
An area of a worksheet that has been highlighted using the mouse for an action or command, such as copy or clear, to be performed on it.

VALUE
See cell value.

WORKBOOK
A collection of worksheets.

WORKSHEET
A grid of cells into which you enter data and then manipulate that data.